GIRL, THERE'S NO EXCUSE.

GIRL, THERE'S NO EXCUSE

"A recession proof entrepreneurial guide to success"

Natalie Birdsong
Keayna Washington
Stephanie Elise

© Copyright 2023, Natalie Birdsong, Keayna Washington, Stephanie Elise

All rights reserved.

No part of this publication may be reproduced, distributed, or transmitted in any form or by any means, including photocopying, recording, or other electronic or mechanical methods, or by any information storage and retrieval system without the prior written permission of the publisher, except in the case of very brief quotations embodied in critical reviews and certain other noncommercial uses permitted by copyright law.

For permission requests, write to the publisher addressed "Attention: Permissions Coordinator," at the address below: JWG Publishing House

980 N Federal Highway, Suite 110 Boca Raton, FL 33432
www.businessstartupacademy.live

Distribution: JWG Publishing House

ISBN 979-8-9866536-7-9

Cover Designed: Business Startup & Marketing Solutions LLC

Printed in the United States of America

Dedicated to women bosses everywhere.

We love you

Table of Contents

SECTION 1

YOU ARE NOT EXEMPT, THERE IS NO EXCUSE
Building and Growing a Business in an Uncertain Economy
by: Natalie Birdsong

Introduction 2
    Girl you're crazy 4
    Rumor VS. Fact 4
    Time To Teach 5
    Better Than Ever 6
    The Three Pillars 7
    Integrity and Character 7
    Hard Work 8
    Spirituality 9
    Never Forget This! 11

SECTION 2

BEING AN EXPERT IN YOUR INDUSTRY
Being an Expert in Your Industry and Creating the Best Business Collaboration
by: Keayna Washington

Introduction. 15
    New Beginnings 19
    How to Be an Expert in Your Industry 24
Pandemic Effects on Businesses 27
    Survival Strategies 27
Business Collaboration for Women 31
    Benefits of Collaboration 33
    Tips and Tricks for Better Collaboration 35
How Your Business Will Be of Benefit to the Community 36

SECTION 3

YOU ARE NOT YOUR MISTAKE. YOU ARE A LIONESS WITH BATTLE SCARS
How to bounce back from personal crisis and make millions.
by: Stephanie Elise

INTRODUCTION 43
   Don't let the floss fool you 44
   The Dreaded Discovery 46
   I Made Trauma My Friend 47
   Rising Above Trauma 48
   Multiple Streams of income 50
   Lesson 1: Know the Industry 50
   Lesson 2: Know When to Pivot 51
   Lesson 3: Seize the Moment 52
   Lesson 4: The Power of Multiplying Your Business 52
   Lesson 5: Don't Be Afraid to Sell Your By-Product 54
   Lesson 6: Look for a Silver Lining 54
   The Lesson 56
   Be The Boss Chic You Were Created to Be 56
   Book Description 62

YOU ARE NOT EXEMPT, THERE IS NO EXCUSE

Building and Growing a Business in an Uncertain Economy

By
Natalie Birdsong

INTRODUCTION

Have you ever wondered why everyone defines success differently? No matter how bold or ambitious your plans are to grow your business, the key to your business's success lies in the mastery of who you are, what you believe in, and what you do. You have to practice and master success to become successful.

Success is just as much about the learning experience and hard work, as it is the end result. In this book, I will show you how you can achieve your dreams and overcome limitations, by maximizing the law of the three pillars.

Success looks different for every individual. The external manifestation of success is not where the real results lie. Similar to the analogy of beauty, success is skin deep.

Introduction

Its root is below the surface, where many do not have access. I hope to use my vast experience, as a successful entrepreneur, to help you gain a greater understanding and realization that each one of us has our own unique super power, enabling us to succeed. We are all exceptional individuals, and when we apply our individual superpowers directly to our calling, our talent, business, profession, and even our community, we are more likely to succeed individually and collectively.

You can win in the midst of chaos. Let's win inspite of, despite of and even in the midst of chaos!

Girl you're crazy!

If someone had told me that the *entire* world would stop functioning because of a virus, I would have called them a liar and told them to cut back on watching television for a while. I might have questioned their sanity, or even suggested that they were losing a grip on reality. As far as I'd known, no one in the past few generations of my life had ever experienced such a thing, so there's no way that could happen…right?

Wrong.

My name is Natalie Birdsong, and I'm the founder and CEO of an international beauty conglomerate that focuses on restoring our customers' hair confidence through impeccable styling and high-quality hair care products. I'm going to tell you how this monumental event (dubbed the "pandemic") changed my life and the course of my business trajectory forever.

RUMOR VS. FACT

To provide context and a time frame, it was February 2020. We'd been hearing rumblings in the news about a virus that originated in China, spreading rampant across all continents. It didn't seem too concerning at first, because our government pacified our fears with promises that "things were under control." I wanted to believe that they were right. Not long afterwards, reports of deaths from the virus started coming in. Our hospitals and medical staff were overwhelmed, and the death toll started rising. We were inundated with daily news updates, and not long after, the government declared that we were in a full-blown pandemic. I could not have predicted the social and economic impact that the pandemic would have on small businesses, specifically, in the beauty industry.

In March 2020, beauty salons, barbershops, and spas were deemed "nonessential" businesses and ordered to shut down operations. I knew that my business model was recession-proof, but I learned very quickly that it wasn't *pandemic-proof*. This was a tremendous blow because I had not saved enough money to be out of work indefinitely. To make matters worse, the price of groceries and toiletries skyrocketed, and I was running through my savings – fast! I knew that I had to do something or face the fact that the pandemic was going to pull me under. It was time to pivot.

TIME TO TEACH

Fortunately, I attended college prior to getting a cosmetology education. Since I was no longer able to operate my salon, I started thinking of new ways to earn income. I reflected on skillsets that I learned working as an advertising executive prior to starting my hair business. I remembered learning about the impact that advertising has on businesses during recessions or unstable economic environments. I also remembered that I was thoroughly trained on how to help small to medium-sized businesses identify their target market audiences and cultivate impactful business messaging that would help attract ideal customers. I knew that in an uncertain economic climate, these particular skillsets were *golden*, and that thousands of businesses would need someone like me to help them reposition themselves to capture new market share. The pandemic had exposed a new set of problems for business owners, and I had the solution…or at least part of it.

I connected with four other businesswomen and combined our skillsets to sell high-ticket digital education products, geared towards providing a solution for business owners that wanted to learn how to attract customers and get profitable. This venture was wildly successful and helped me stay buoyant over the few months that my business was closed. In June 2020, beauty businesses were allowed to reopen.

BETTER THAN EVER

No one could have prepared me for the psychological impact that the pandemic would have on the beauty industry. You see, for *months*, people were restricted from indulging in basic beauty maintenance, such as hair appointments, grooming appointments, nail appointments, spa appointments, etc. This created a frenzy for those services once those beauty businesses opened back up. My salon became busier than it had ever been, and my schedule stayed booked with both new and existing clients.

In all transparency, things were great…except for one minor detail. I had a business partner that was the co-owner of the salon, and we decided to end the business relationship. This presented a new problem, because we were still in a lease and had not prepared to prematurely dissolve the business. To add fuel to the fire, our landlord was pressing us for back-rent, accrued during the months that our business was not allowed to operate. Eventually, they took us to court, and we settled on an amount that resolved the matter.

We officially closed the doors to that salon on June 30, 2022, and eight days later, I opened the doors to my very own salon home, the Hair by Natalie B. Salon. Today, my business portfolio includes that beautiful, upscale salon, advanced hair care products, premium ethnic-friendly hair extensions, and educational courses for hairstylists looking to refine their skillset and business offerings. I've been invited to share my story on panels, podcasts, and at high-level business events. I am currently a cast member on a reality show that showcases my life as a beauty entrepreneur. My brand has gained notoriety globally, and I am one of Chicago's most sought-after hairstylists. I've worked on celebrities, and my work has been featured in major publications like Ebony, and on major television networks like VH1. I've been recognized as an Influential Business Leader in Chicago and have earned numerous awards for my efforts in this industry and as a small business owner

My success has not been accidental or a fluke. I've followed a specific set of principles to help guide my efforts and decision-making, and I have no doubt in my mind that these principles saved me in that pandemic. I call them the Three Pillars.

THE THREE PILLARS

I've found that life's most difficult challenges can be overcome by focusing on three areas of life. They are Integrity and Character, Hard Work, and Spirituality. I often refer to these three areas as the Three Pillars, and in order to be successful, all three areas must be full.

INTEGRITY AND CHARACTER

My father once told me that if I lost everything I had in this world that I should be able to rebuild my life, leaning on my good name. In other words, if I lost all my money and all my material possessions, others should be encouraged to help me because of my impeccable character and reputation. You see, in life, we have no control of the circumstances that we are born into, only the outcome. How you handle people and hardships that you endure showcase your strengths and flaws. Are you trustworthy? Are you known for taking care of your family and handling your business? Are you viewed as a leader among your peers, and can others count on you?

I was invited to join that group of businesswomen during the pandemic because my reputation for having good character and integrity attracted that opportunity. If I had cultivated a reputation for being shady in business dealings, or being a liar or a thief, or someone that a team couldn't depend on, that opportunity would have surely passed me by. Before you decide how you'll handle a situation or a person, ask yourself if that decision will add to or take away from your character. Be dependable, keep your word, and tell the truth.

HARD WORK

This one should be a no-brainer, but you'd be surprised how many people expect you to do their dirty work for them!

Building and growing a business requires you to invest endless hours into learning and mastering that business, and refining your skillsets, constantly, along the way. There isn't a shortcut to gaining the experience needed to be proficient in your industry. I'm often asked if someone can "pick my brain" or help them get their business off the off the ground. While I genuinely enjoy helping people grow their businesses, I always encourage them to do their own research first.

YouTube is full of free information and tutorials, Google is an endless source of data, and experience is the best teacher, so you must be willing to try a few things to see what works and what doesn't. Refusal to do any of these actions translates as lazy, and no one wants to help someone who won't help themselves.

When they closed my business during the pandemic, I knew that pivoting to support my current lifestyle would be difficult because my monthly expenses were high. I experienced a learning curve with digital products because I had never created any before. I had to learn how to write and record an online course, and I'm not technology-savvy. I spent days on end scouring the internet for information that I could add to my product to make it more robust and informative. I relied on video tutorials on YouTube to teach me how to successfully do a voice-over so that I could create customized audio for the digital product. I consulted with my colleagues on best practices for creating a profitable product. I left no stone unturned, because I knew that if this didn't work, I was doomed, and eventually, it *did* work.

You can't be afraid to roll up your sleeves and dive in. Playing it safe rarely keeps you safe, and no one is coming to save you from yourself.

SPIRTUALITY

This last pillar is the most controversial of the three but is also the most important. If you listen to nothing else that I

Spirituality

tell you, listen to this, success is spiritual, and your success is locked up in your obedience to following the moral roadmap and operating with good intention.

Regardless of your religion or belief system, believing in something higher than yourself establishes a roadmap to morality, standards, and good character. When this roadmap is cast aside, chaos ensues, and your emotional, mental, and spiritual stability become out of balance.

The pandemic forced many of us to spend time alone, with our thoughts and ourselves. Many of us reexamined our priorities, and our relationships with others, even our spiritual relationships. The idea of being a "good person" echoes throughout religious doctrines and showing gratitude and giving thanks for even the tiniest of blessings opens the door for even more greatness to come your way.

Your beliefs create energy, and that energy either attracts or repels people, places, and things to you. In my most challenging or darkest hours, I rely on my spiritual connection with God to see me through and over those obstacles. I am intentional about remaining grateful and calling out loud the things that I am grateful for.

This practice may be awkward for those who are not accustomed to doing so. To help organize your thoughts, you can purchase a gratitude journal, which offers a guided experience to capturing those thoughts.

Remember to speak affirming thoughts over your life, because no one speaks louder than the voice in your head, and it's listening to everything that you say about yourself.

NEVER FORGET THIS!

Opportunity knocks once. Distraction leans on the doorbell. I made it out of the pandemic with my business intact and my mentality stronger than ever. I use the Three Pillars as a checkpoint to make sure that I'm staying on task. Today, I am focusing on growing a multi-million-dollar brand and helping others overcome hair insecurities and business insecurities.

TAKE SOME TIME TO REFLECT ON THIS SECTION AND NOTATE SOME ACTIONABLE POINTS

Where can we connect?

To follow my journey, connect with me on Instagram at @iamhairbynatalieb, or visit me online at www.nataliebirdsong.com.

"The best way to predict the future is to create it."

~Natalie B.

Thanks again for your support!

BEING AN EXPERT IN YOUR INDUSTRY

Being an Expert in Your Industry and Creating the Best Business Collaboration

By
Keayna Washington

INTRODUCTION

You've spent years building the knowledge that has made you successful, whether you're a one-person consulting firm or a two-hundred-fifty-person manufacturing operation. Why not make the most of your expertise by using it to establish authority or even superstar status in your industry?

That's exactly what I did. I am Keayna Washington, the serial entrepreneur. Many wonder how I do it. As a mortgage broker owner-operator, certified credit consultant, business financial advisor, author, podcaster, food truck operator, and most importantly, mother. Well, the answer is easy. **Systems**!

Introduction

Every new business venture I would start I made sure that I learned the business forwards and backwards. I learned how to operate within my business as a worker as well as the owner and the boss. Once I mastered the two, I was able to put systems in place that allowed me to wear the many hats that I wear today.

In my eyes, there is no business too big and no business too small. Wealth is to be obtained, and it's up to you to go out and grab it. So, I did just that. In 2016, I decided I wanted to next-level my credit knowledge to have the ability to help others after running into a credit issue for the second time.

The first time was in 2006 when I learned that I had a negative collection account on my credit report that I was not responsible for that hindered me from getting my first apartment.

Imagine being an eighteen-year-old responsible adult who was eager to be grown. That was me. I was that girl. I was fresh out of high school. I was considered a teen mom, and I was so excited to say that I would have my own apartment. It was a low-income housing project, so there was no doubt in my mind that I wouldn't be approved. To learn that my credit didn't suffice crushed me. At that very moment was when my credit education journey began.

I remember going to my mom asking how could this be only to learn that my mom was responsible for the negative account reporting. I knew well enough to know that I was unable to obtain any form of credit rightfully prior to the age of eighteen. I sought advice and was directed to the credit bureaus. TransUnion, Equifax, and Experian – and that was my first encounter with credit. I was able to successfully get the item removed and started building my credit from there on out.

Fast forward to the year 2016. I was ready to become a first-time home buyer, and I was ready to get to the tables and obtain a pre-approval. I had been working in mortgage banking for quite some time and knew the mortgage process forwards and backwards.

"This my year." Everything that I had been working hard for was about to come to surface. I was really about to be on my own. It was time for us to get to the closing table, but there was no closing that was going to take place.

If you know anything about the mortgage process, when your initial mortgage application is done, your credit is pulled to determine your credit-worthiness. Also prior to signing CDs (closing disclosure) another credit report is pulled to ensure you still meet the qualifications. Once my second pull was done, I learned my scores had dropped drastically.

Yes, I knew the basics of credit and what credit consisted of, but I did not know the process of how utilization, mixed credit, payment history, and inquires affected your overall scoring. During the homebuying process, I decided to go purchase a new car, not knowing that would affect my mortgage approval.

Introduction

Long story short, I was left shattered. I did not close, and I became very discouraged about trying to move forward with the home-buying process. Maybe it just wasn't my time. It was like I was reliving 2006 all over again. I had gotten so excited about being able to take life to the next level. Becoming a homeowner was considered a big deal where I'm from.

Back to the drawing board. I was not going to allow insufficient credit to defeat me. Or deter me from getting the things that I wanted and deserved in life. I was introduced to one of Chicago's reputable credit repair guys. I remember setting up a consult for service. He was very impressed with the knowledge I possessed in reference to credit and home loans. He immediately tried convincing me to join his team. Immediately, I declined. I was not fond of the idea of offering credit repair services to individuals for profit. I had been working in corporate America so long and studying paralegal studies that anything less didn't make sense to me.

Eventually, I enrolled into his program for the credit repair services. I got results instantly. It was almost like he had a magic wand. I was intrigued. I wanted in. I wanted to be able to help my family and friends obtain good credit.

The results that I was getting was mind blowing. I went from a 622 to a 750 credit score in a matter of months. I needed to know how he made that possible. I wasn't willing to be a team member, but I was willing to pay the cost to learn the process. In a matter of months, I became proficient enough

Introduction

to where I was willing to take clients who needed my assistance. As results came in, my interests grew higher and higher. I went from one client to sixty. I went from beginner to expert. I created a side hustle from my expertise in credit. I made hundreds and thousands of dollars effortlessly. My mission was to provide individuals with knowledge and accessibility in a pursuit of a home-buying goal and business startup.

Shortly after mastering the credit industry, I started real estate school. I had been working in mortgage banking for eight years and knew all aspects of back-end real estate. Tapping into the front-end process would for sure make me a pillar in the industry.

New Beginnings

In 2018, I was surprised with the gift of being a mom of two twelve years later. My family was ecstatic. The only thing that ran through my mind was obtaining greater financial stability. I knew that bringing a new kid in the world would require me to have greater responsibilities, and with greater responsibilities comes greater financial obligations. I had vowed to give my son the world, but now I had to vow to give my children the world. At that very moment, I knew I wanted more. More than what I was already working to accomplish. That year, I decided to take a leap out on faith. I asked God to guide my steps and lead the way. I wanted to become a full-time entrepreneur. I was scared, but I had to give it a try.

I wanted this mommy experience to be different. I was given the chance to be a mom again, and this time, I was a mature adult. I remember giving my employer my thirty-day notice. I didn't know exactly how it was going to go, but I knew that with faith as small as a mustard seed that I would succeed. This new journey was personal.

Instantly, I began to search for an office space to go live as a credit repair company. I had gained the trust of so many people that expansion was necessary. During my new journey, I faced many obstacles, let downs and heartbreaks. Nevertheless, I didn't allow it to break me. I kept going. I eventually found an office space that I fell in love with. It was nine hundred dollars over my seven-hundred-dollar budget, but something in me allowed me to be a risk taker.

I was due to get the keys to my new business space on April 15, 2019. That weekend was filled with many festivities for me. I was giving the opportunity to participate in the Black Women's Expo of Chicago. To be a part of such a huge event in the Chicago metropolitan area was everything to me. Having the ability to display myself to so many people of different origins and background was next level for KNA. Sunday, April 14, 2019, my family, and I had a large gathering to celebrate my son's first birthday and my new business. We were on to new beginnings.

Life Changing

At 1:10 a.m., I got a call from my grandmother telling me my father had been hospitalized, and he wasn't going to make it. I thought to myself, *"How could this be?"* I had spoken to him over the weekend, and everything was fine. My whole world was turned upside down.

I remember calling the hospital, and the nurse told me that a doctor would be in contact with me first thing in the morning.

The very next morning around 9:30 a.m., I received a call from the doctor, who explained to me the condition of my father. She later let me know that my father was not going to make it, and the machines were working for him. I cried and pleaded with the doctor to do everything she could to keep him here. She let me know that there was nothing else that could be done. I was crushed. My word hasn't been the same since my biggest supporter would no longer be there to see his princess excel.

I was facing the lowest moments in life, but I was also striving to reach my highest potential in business. While grieving the loss of my father, I managed to reach my highest peak in business. Like any other businessowner, I was scared to open and start a new business, wondering if I would be able to afford it on a consistent basis. Wondering if I would have sufficient clientele. I knew I owed it to myself and my father. I was eager to win! I was eager to grow. I was eager to lead by example, not only for my family, but for those who were watching.

Just as I began to finally ease up and find some joy and comfort in my new role, we were faced with a life-changing global crisis known as COVID-19. In January 2020, the world had learned of the outbreak of a severe respiratory infection. By March of 2020, it was declared a pandemic. Not even one year after opening my doors, I was forced to close them due to a mandated order. The entire world was in an uproar. We didn't know what was coming our way. Who would it affect? Was it deadly? How did we prevent getting this contagious infection? What happened now that the world was closed? What could we do to survive?

While the world was trying to figure out the whys, I began to focus on the *now*. I knew that the *now* was crucial. Whether you were an entrepreneur or worked in corporate America. Whether you were black, white, or brown. Whether you were rich or poor. Everyone was facing the pandemic.

If you had never gotten in front of your finances, now was the time. It was the time to do financial planning and budgeting, keeping hard-earned cash in your pocket and utilizing available credit sources. My message was "If you don't know the importance of credit, now is the time. Credit dictates so much of your financial freedom and gives you the ability to buy the things you need, so it is time to take control of your *now* in order for us to have a better tomorrow." I knew that too shall pass, and a recovery plan would be crucial.

As we were experiencing this world pandemic, it was important for me to share my knowledge and accessibility. I didn't know what to expect of the COVID-19 virus, but what I did know was due to mandated world order and the closures of businesses and loss of jobs. Credit would be monumental during these trying times. My message had reached hundreds of people and while everyone else's business was suffering, mine was thriving. I went from 109 clients to 550 clients. At that moment, there was no looking back. I had created my authority.

Once you've established yourself as an authority or expert in your industry, it leads to other business opportunities and having the ability to expand your business and accelerate your success. In today's environment, can anyone truly understand what it means to be an expert? Whatever business you operate in, there will always be fierce competition. The most important thing is to make oneself stand out to get the results you seek. Remember: if you want to become an expert in your field, learn everything you can about your job and the industry you work in and keep learning throughout your career.

Developing an expert reputation in your field is an art form; you can stand out from the crowd by applying self-marketing and personal branding. By compiling your information and incorporating it into your overall package, you will be able to reach out to a broader audience while also establishing new systems that will lead to increased revenues.

One of the advantages of becoming an expert in your field is that you will be exposed to many opportunities that will expand your sources of wealth. Being an expert entails acquiring a professional reputation, which leads to a cascade of success much beyond your wildest dreams.

As of April 2022, business was back to normal, and it was now time to move on to bigger and better. I am proud to announce that I am an independent Illinois residential mortgage company. Being exposed to wider audiences, I was able to comfortably create bigger avenues for myself. I was encouraged to create higher significance of service for the people and birthed KNA Mortgage Brokerage. (The full story is detailed in my book *Knowledge and Accessibility of Credit*).

I have learned once you've mastered your craft, you'll need to make plans for some big lifestyle changes. Traveling around the world should be high on your to-do list at this time because you will be getting more and more knowledge while freely exposing yourself to a much more diverse population.

Your branding will naturally improve once you've established yourself as an authority in your field. You will find that you have more time to accomplish the things you enjoy and more time to spend with your family and friends as a side benefit.

It is satisfying in and of itself to know that you have had an impact on someone else's life. As you strengthen your branding, you will begin to enjoy a more stress-free and meaningful existence due to your expert status.

How to Be an Expert in Your Industry

Becoming a renowned expert in your field is a process that does not happen by itself. You must take a proactive approach that includes ongoing education and networking with key people in your field. You may create your reputation and position yourself as a reputable authority in your field by maintaining a consistent focus and dedication. The ten steps to becoming a renowned expert in your field are outlined here.

Showcase Your Industry Knowledge

One of the most prevalent characteristics among wellknown industry specialists is their enthusiasm to share their knowledge with others. You can follow suit by demonstrating your understanding of the industry in the following ways:

Showcase Your Industry Knowledge

- Volunteer to speak at a community event
- Write an e-book on a topic you're passionate about

Attend Industry Trade Shows

Trade exhibitions provide numerous opportunities to demonstrate your abilities while networking with business leaders. Whether you participate as an exhibitor or a walk-around participant, you can expand your knowledge in the following ways:

- Gain access to the most cutting-edge approaches used in your profession
- Network with major leaders in your field

Become A Mentor

Serving as a mentor to newcomers in your field benefits both you and those you're coaching. When you share your expertise with individuals who need it, you accomplish the four goals below, which will help you cement your reputation as a recognized expert. Prior to starting KNA Elite Mentor, I had no desire to offer such a service. I felt that I offered a lot with my public information. Mentoring took me and my brand to another level. Everyone wanted the exclusive intel.

- Mentoring helps you establish yourself as a credible expert in your subject.
- Sharing your knowledge and talents validates what you already know.
- You broaden your current knowledge base.
- As a professional, your worth rises.

Start A Blog

Starting a blog is an excellent method to demonstrate your expertise while also interacting with others in your profession. Although starting a blog is free, you should ensure that you have the time and resources to provide new content regularly. Here are some keynotes to help you create a blog that will help you establish yourself as an authority in your field:

- Choose themes that are both intriguing and relevant to your field's audience.
- Always proofread your work for spelling and grammatical problems and write properly.
- Respond to comments and queries about your blog from readers.

Voice Your Educated Opinion

When your reputation as an industry expert grows, people will expect you to have an opinion and make recommendations based on that opinion. You may increase your credibility by expressing your thoughts as long as you back them up with facts, studies, and discoveries. Because of this, I started my podcast *Knowledge and Accessibility*, where we talk all things credit and home loans.

Use Social Media

On an average, a person will spend about five years of their lives on social networking. You can reach thousands of like-minded people in your field via social media. You may use favorable social media comments to highlight your accomplishments because eighty-four percent of people trust online evaluations as much as they would a personal referral.

PANDEMIC EFFECTS ON BUSINESSES

The COVID-19 pandemic has exposed many vulnerabilities and capabilities amongst us all. Overall, in my view, during the crisis you either won or lost. While many businesses sunk, I thrived for higher. I knew people needed me more than ever. Something sparked inside of me. It was like God ignited a fire that was flaming. The more I was able to help people during such a trying time, the more power I got. I was awakened by my purpose. I am not just a businesswoman. "I *am* the business." My life isn't about my personal gains. My life is purposeful in the service of others.

Survival Strategies

Businesses, no matter how well-established, are still facing significant challenges and are being forced to rethink how they manage and execute their operations, including revisiting their business plans. So, when something as significant as this occurs, it can be devastating not only for the small business owner but also for the employees who rely on them. So, how can businesses weather the storms? There is no simple fix, but here are some ideas to start implementing and planning for your next chapter.

Don't panic, take care of yourself, and keep calm.

This might be challenging, especially when money is tight, but remember to look after yourself in a way that works for you: eat healthily and get some exercise, for example.

Taking care of yourself helps you stay peaceful, resulting in a healthy mindset for everyone to come up with new ideas to go forward. If you're presented with a difficult choice, take some time to center yourself and your mind before making a final decision. In a scenario that is very dynamic and fast-changing, taking a step back to reassess, seek reputable viewpoints, and maintain perspective can all help. Things will improve, and you are not alone in this.

Maintain transparent communication with your customers.

I ensured my customers that we're all in this together. Therefore, the best thing you can do is to keep your customers informed about what your company is going through. Customers can empathize with businesses in distress if the communication is open and honest. Communicate with customers to learn about their opinions on your product or service.

Keeping a positive relationship with contracted parties.

It's logical that paying merchants and suppliers can be tough during shutdown. However, it would be beneficial to give your vendors, suppliers, landlords, and others prior notice in the event of a payment delay so that they can be prepared, and animosity is avoided during this already tough time. Tap into resources provided by the government and financial institutions. Governments worldwide are putting together efforts to help small business owners, which is something that is constantly changing. Keep up to date on

Financial plan & opportunities

how your government and other vital organizations such as banks with a social duty can assist.

Make a three-month financial plan.

Employees pay, office rent, and utility bills are some of the most common expenses for small businesses.

Talk to the people you need to pay in the next three months (landlord and suppliers and see what options you have for spreading the costs out. Because it is in their best interest to keep your business, they may already have choices in place or will be understanding. Always be cautious when negotiating payment plans with other small businesses, as they, too, are trying to stay afloat; therefore, this should be a win-win situation for both of you.

Examine your finances and chat with anyone who can help you develop a realistic plan for controlling your spending for the next three months. What expenses are necessary, and what can be postponed? If you have a partner helping you expand your business as the breadwinner, have an open and honest conversation with them about your short and long-term business goals.

Find the opportunities.

It's never a good idea to profit from incidents like this, but they can also serve as a wake-up call to reassess your business practices. Is your company model capable of surviving the alterations brought on by crisis or downfalls? Is it possible for you to digitize any of your products or services and sell them online? Can you use technology to offset potential revenue losses by providing new methods to operate?

Upskill your staff.

Try to maintain your employees if at all feasible; they rely on you, and if you've built a successful team, they should be rooting for you. Rather than recruiting more people, you could teach your current employees new skills, making them more productive and efficient.

During trying times, it's critical that we stick together and aid one another in every way we can. Keep yourself safe and healthy. Please keep in mind that some of the most successful projects are born out of adversity. This, like all terrible situations, will pass! *You* are the business!

BUSINESS COLLABORATION FOR WOMEN

Collaboration refers to the intentional efforts as entrepreneurs to improve the world, form deep bonds, and grow our collective learning. Do you, on the other hand, find yourself avoiding cooperation to prevent drama? Or perhaps you're an introvert who finds chatting to strangers a little unsettling. In business, collaboration is essential. On the other hand, working with other people is difficult; yet it is rewarding when you succeed. Collaboration is a strong tool for growing and strengthening your company.

In business, as in life, you grow via your contacts, ideas, and creativity. Collaboration is powerful in today's world for any organization or business, and when done well, it can propel your company to new heights.

If you're a woman entrepreneur who hasn't started collaborating yet, keep reading to see why you should. It was always necessary to work in groups and have social skills when you are a community member. Social abilities help you stand out, particularly in the commercial industry.

A healthy rivalry is ingrained in today's corporate world, but is it always the greatest approach to business? Society places a great priority on community and connection, thanks in part to social media. Collaboration as a wise business strategy emerges as a result of this change away from an ultra-competitive environment.

Is it feasible that collaboration, rather than rivalry, can lead to better commercial results? I prefer to believe so, especially when it comes to women-owned enterprises.

The present figures on the difficulties women face in the workplace aren't encouraging – they're a wake-up call. Gender bias, "old boys clubs," salary disparities, and societal standards persist in places, and they often disadvantage women.

How do we get through these engrained and daunting obstacles? Partnerships must be embraced as part of the answer. Collaborative, win-win connections may help founders expand faster, create new opportunities, and build a network of supporters to get them through difficult times.

Finding the appropriate companions, on the other hand, can be difficult and frightening. "What if someone takes my idea?" the little voice in the back of your mind fears. "What if they steal my clients?"

On the other hand, true collaboration is built on trust and loyalty, which should assuage these misgivings. The truth is that no one can scale a business on their own, no matter how clever or talented they are.

A network of supporters, confidants, partners, and mentors surrounds every outstanding CEO and corporate leader. After all, the best leaders don't rely solely on their abilities. They see their flaws because they are self-aware. They understand as leaders that forming alliances to fill those gaps is a wise business option.

Benefits of Collaboration

Collaboration with other women may seem strange in today's competitive society, but things aren't always unpleasant. Collaboration and business can occasionally go hand in hand, just like each coin has two sides.

We are, without a doubt, in a period of rivalry, but we are also in a period of growth. There will be times when we cannot discover a solution, but teamwork and collaboration may be able to assist us. After all, you need input for all of your efforts in your industry, which is only achievable if you've partnered with other professional ladies. People with different core talents can assist you in your business in a variety of ways:

It helps you know your strength and weaknesses.

Working with other women might help you become more aware of your strengths and flaws. We are all born with certain characteristics and, at the same time, some flaws. Collaboration allows us to reflect and learn more about ourselves. Self-awareness is essential not only for personal development but also for the success of our company. Only by cooperating will you be able to identify your strengths and weaknesses and the issues that need to be addressed.

It helps your solve problems effectively.

Getting stuck in a dilemma and attempting to solve it on your own will take time. However, if you have another person's assistance, support, or guidance, you are more likely to solve the problem quickly and more efficiently. When you combine your core abilities with the experiences and talents of others and other resources such as funds and infrastructure, you may efficiently address business-related difficulties.

It helps you to be innovative.

In today's business world, innovation is a prerequisite for your company's existence. Customers nowadays are looking for something new and exciting. In a matter of days or months, whatever is introduced today will be obsolete. You learn to be innovative when you network with others. You learn new things and come up with new ideas, which you can apply to your business to boost its growth and take it to the next level.

It helps you learn new things.

My participation in this book as an author was based upon collaboration. I was introduced to co-authors Natalie Birdsong and Stephanie Elise through my brand manager, Que Johnson. Now here we are two years later, and I'm so ever grateful to call these ladies my big sisters. Sharing this platform with the two has been one for the books – literally. Collaborating with others has encouraged me to learn more. When you network with people and step outside of your comfort zone, you learn and grow, and your business will benefit as a result.

Tips and Tricks for Better Collaboration
Keep your eyes on the goal.
Never lose sight of the goal that you're all aiming for. Make

that point your true north for all decisions, tactics, and activities. When things grow unclear or difficult, assist your colleagues in staying the course. Detours might be beneficial, but they usually lead you further away from your destination.

Extend trust first.

We don't always have a say in who we collaborate with. It can happen with people we don't know, or even worse, people we don't like or are unsure of. Forget about the rumors and the gossip. Give others the benefit of the doubt and put your faith first. It's surprising how a simple act of extending trust can break down barriers and spark wonderful long-term partnerships. Remember, we have no idea what obstacles others are facing in the background.

Know what you're good at and what you're weaker at.

Make a list of your assets. Examine your weaknesses objectively. Make the most of your assets and seek treatment for your weaknesses. Both are present in all of us. Take on the duties that you can easily complete. Volunteer for the organizations that will assist you in your development. Suppose you've been given a task that you know you'll fail at, then you should enlist the support of a co-worker. There's a chance that someone else is in the same boat as you. It's better to have two (or more) heads than one. Collaboration's genius is that it allows you to pool your talents to complete the task.

Be willing to help and be helped.

When someone asks you for assistance, give it to them. Help them, especially if you don't know what to do. When you take on anything new, you'll be surprised at how much you learn about yourself and your co-worker. That is also true in reverse. Don't be frightened to seek assistance. Don't say no to anyone who offers to assist you. The strongest relationships are formed as a result of these exchanges.

Turn off your sarcasm channel.

Make no doubt about it. Sarcasm is rage that has been masked. You're venting your frustrations on others when you make a caustic remark. It's a form of passive-aggressive conduct that benefits no one, particularly you. It isn't kind. It makes it impossible to have fruitful discourse.

How Your Business Will Be of Benefit to the Community

Your companies have a greater impact on others than you may realize. Many major enterprises cannot represent a community's character and interact with their neighbors on a business and personal level. Celebrating a small business entail more than just praising its eccentric or hipster clientele; it also entails recognizing and appreciating the positive impact it has on your community and local government, as well as all of the independent and unique products or services that aren't available from large corporations.

Local Jobs

As the number of small enterprises grows, so does the number of available jobs. Local employment is great since they limit the number of time employees spend traveling and commuting to work. Your area's unemployment rate may begin to decline by creating local jobs, resulting in positive economic impacts.

You can boost job opportunities at other neighboring small businesses and add local positions within the small businesses. People are more inclined to shop around from one business to the next in a dynamic community with small companies scattered throughout, rather than going to one department store for everything they need. Small firms require additional staff to be productive as their visibility grows.

Increase Tax Base

Small enterprises provide tax revenue, which is then re-invested in the local economy, resulting in a more prosperous community. This implies that your school districts, police departments, and other small businesses and organizations will form a support network and benefit from one another's efforts.

Less Infrastructure and Low Maintenance

Small enterprises do not necessitate as much effort and upkeep as a major organization. These small businesses can be added to existing buildings because they are generally located in the heart of a city or the downtown region. This has a favorable impact on the economy since it reduces the amount of city planning that needs to be done. It also takes less time and effort than planning and developing a new mall or department store.

Product Diversity

A small business's responsibility is to be inventive, new, and diversified. In general, an independent business will offer unique products that are not available at larger merchants.

Small firms can collaborate with other companies. Many items can be manufactured using the commodities and services of other local businesses, allowing earnings to be reinvested in the community. Technology can also help your business succeed, particularly when it comes to internet buying.

TAKE SOME TIME TO REFLECT ON THIS SECTION AND NOTATE SOME ACTIONABLE POINTS

_____

_____

_____

_____

_____

_____

_____

_____

_____

_____

_____

_____

_____

_____

_____

_____

Disclaimer

This portion of the book is not intended as a substitute for the practical experience but as a guide. The reader should regularly consult a business counsellor if you notice something going wrong.

Do Not Go Yet! One Last Thing to Do:

If you enjoyed this book or found it useful, I'd be very grateful if you'd post a short review on Amazon. Your support does make a difference, and I read all the reviews personally so I can get your feedback and make this book even better.

Also, check out my credit education book *Knowledge and Accessibility of Credit* to learn all things credit and business finance.

Be sure to tune in to my podcast *Knowledge and Accessibility* that's available on Apple Music, Pandora, Amazon Audible, Spotify and Iheart.

Connect with me on Instagram at @keaynaw_ or visit me online at
https://linktr.ee/keaynawashington

Thanks again for your support!

YOU ARE NOT YOUR MISTAKE. YOU ARE A LIONESS WITH BATTLE SCARS.

How to bounce back from personal crisis and make millions

By
Stephanie Elise

INTRODUCTION

Life is a journey, and like any journey, it has its ups and downs. But it's not the bumps in the road that define us, it's how we choose to navigate them that determines our destination". - Unknown

Are you tired of feeling like your mistakes define you? Do you feel like your personal life is hindering your entrepreneurial success? As an entrepreneur, it's easy to get caught up in the illusion of perfection portrayed on social media. But the truth is, life is messy, and relationships can be complicated.

Introduction

As someone who has battled personal crises while building a successful business, I can tell you that it's possible to bounce back and thrive. It starts with:

- Prioritizing yourself
- Setting strict boundaries
- Practicing time management
- Reviewing relationships
- Choosing yourself repeatedly
- Surrounding yourself with the right people
- Mastering effective communication

But let's be real, these are easier said than done. That's why I'm here to share my story and show you that you are not defined by your mistakes. Let's take a walk together and discover how you too can overcome personal struggles and achieve entrepreneurial greatness. Are you ready to take control of your personal and professional life? Let's do this together. Remember, you are a lioness with battle scars, and it's time to roar louder than ever before.

Don't let the floss fool you.
I can still remember when Covid hit. During that time, I made the most income in my business. While it was bad financially for a lot of people, that was not my reality. Do you know what my reality was? I had an abundance of wealth, but I was complacent in my relationship, settling for less than what I truly desired.

You may say, as an entrepreneur, why not talk about business? I believe in order to lead in business, we have to be healed in our personal lives in real life. I want my chapters in this book to be raw and vulnerable as I share about the effects of mental and domestic abuse. If I can help somebody with what I have gone through, then it will be worth it for me.

Many people know me as the confident woman who knows how to find ways to make money. Many individuals are unaware of the fact that I experience challenges with a speech disorder. As a result of this condition, I encounter difficulty when it comes to articulating my words clearly like the majority of people do. Furthermore, this has made it challenging for me to convey my ideas or express myself effectively. I have always felt uneasy in situations where I have to speak out loud, especially in large crowds. This discomfort also carried over to my home environment, leading me to avoid speaking up and settling for less.

I found myself in a relationship with a guy who was not the type I usually go for, but I thought to myself, I'm at a certain age where I need to start building and growing with a partner. My businesses were thriving, and I felt it was time to focus on improving my love life as well.

When we struggle with our mental and emotional well-being, it can be challenging to prioritize ourselves in our relationships. Our focus may be on seeking validation and approval from others, or we may struggle with feelings of inadequacy and low self-worth. This can lead us to neglect our own needs and desires, putting the needs of others first. Over time, this can erode our sense of self and leave us \feeling drained and resentful. In order to cultivate healthy relationships, it's essential to prioritize our own self-care and emotional well-being. This may involve seeking therapy or support from trusted friends and family members, practicing self-compassion and self-love, and setting healthy boundaries with others. By prioritizing our own needs and emotional health, we can build stronger, more fulfilling relationships with others. When we begin practicing these small but impactful changes, they begin to manifest not only in our personal lives but in business as well.

The Dreaded Discovery

I was making plans to attend a mastermind conference where I was going to be recognized for my achievements in Vegas when I received a message that changed everything. The message read, "My boyfriend XXX said that you guys are friends, but he will not let me meet you, and I don't understand what the big deal is about us meeting." It turned out that the boyfriend that this young lady was texting me about, was the man I once lived with, who I was trying to work things out with, yes, he was my boyfriend as well.

I called her right away, and we talked for hours. As we compared notes, we realized that we had both been two-timed by the same man. Looking back, I think my intense focus on making money may have contributed to the breakdown of our relationship. I had low self-worth, and even after he moved out, I was watching his kids, helping him fix his credit to buy a house, and trying to work things out because I didn't want to fail again. After much self- reflection, many tears, and a few glasses of wine, I realized I was doing it again; Settling for less with a man who wasn't my equal and did not deserve me, to avoid failure. Little did I know I had failed long before that when I chose him and allowed him into my life.

All of this was happening during the Covid pandemic, and a major life transition was about to happen. The young lady and I decided to confront him right before I flew to Vegas, but of course, he lied through his teeth. I was exhausted mentally and emotionally from settling for less. Did I mention that I had met his lying tail after coming out of a physically abusive marriage? This is what trauma does, it chooses for us.

I Made Trauma my Friend.

The abuse started just three weeks into my marriage in 2009, and despite the physical and verbal abuse, I stayed in the marriage for seven years. I was more concerned about what others would think of me if my relationship failed, than my own safety and well-being. It wasn't until years later that I found the courage to leave my abuser.

Leaving the abusive relationship was a difficult decision, but necessary for my own safety and well-being. However, after leaving, I was left feeling broken and defeated. I decided to focus on my finances but failed to address the root cause of my trauma, resulting in a pattern of being cheated on in subsequent relationships.

Despite my struggles, I continued to fight feelings of failure and disappointment. I didn't want to be seen as a victim or a failure in my marriage. However, I knew that staying in an abusive relationship was not an option, and over time, it caused me to feel inadequate, unattractive, and unworthy.

I never lost hope in love, but my priorities shifted towards creating more profit. In 2014, I embarked on a mission to establish other streams of income and founded Pretty Girls Waisted, a business that specializes in waist trainers, aiding products, and body contouring services. This became my third stream of income and business. However, the pandemic made me realize that I needed to diversify my offerings to sustain my business's growth.

I Made Trauma my Friend

In 2021, I was introduced to a health and wellness company based in Vegas that offered supplements and other products through a business contact. My newfound business contact reached out to me in my inbox and introduced me to the company. I knew it was meant to be because I had just prayed for guidance on adding new income streams a few nights before. Without hesitation, I joined the company overnight to generate more income. Despite my struggles with depression and uncertainty in my love life, I quickly climbed the ranks, ultimately becoming a top affiliate generating $50,000 in income within a short span of time.

This newfound partnership not only boosted my income but also improved my leadership skills. I became more confident in speaking which bolstered my confidence in building professional relationships. As my business continued to thrive, I sought out like-minded individuals and began to surround myself with multimillionaires who shared my positive outlook and entrepreneurial spirit. This experience taught me the power of networking and the significance of continuously pursuing new opportunities for growth and expansion. Despite not having a fairy tale love life, my focus on myself, and my own personal growth began to reflect in my businesses. There was an increase in my profits which allowed me to expand my business.

The expansion included adding health and wellness products and supplements, which yielded immense personal satisfaction. My opportunities were aligning with my journey personally and professionally. I was no longer in survival mode. I was thriving, dedicating myself to both personal and professional growth, which enabled me to flourish even in trying times.

Rising Above Trauma

Trauma can have a lasting impact on our lives, especially

when it comes to our relationships and entrepreneurial pursuits. I know this from personal experience. The abuse I endured in my marriage left me with emotional scars that took years to heal. But healing is possible, and it's essential if we want to build healthy relationships and successful businesses. For a long time, I felt like a victim, and it seemed like my trauma was in control of my life. It affected how I saw myself, my ability to trust others, and my capacity for joy. I struggled with anxiety and depression, and it was challenging to focus on anything else. It wasn't until I started seeking help that I began to see a way out of my pain.

Therapy was a game-changer for me. It provided me with the tools I needed to process my trauma, understand how it was impacting my life, and develop strategies to move forward. I learned how to set boundaries, prioritize my needs, and communicate effectively with others. These skills were essential in both my personal and professional life.

I also found solace in my faith. As I leaned on God, I began to realize that I was not alone in my struggles. I started to see myself as a survivor instead of a victim. This shift in mindset was powerful. It gave me the strength to take control of my life and start pursuing my dreams with confidence. Through my healing journey, I discovered that trauma can be a teacher. It can teach us about resilience, strength, and the power of community. It can also teach us about the importance of self-care, boundaries, and healthy relationships.

For example, growing up, I saw the strength and perseverance of my mother who worked a full- time job and had a side hustle to take care of my sister and me. Her example showed me that we have the power to take control of our lives and be proactive in finding solutions to our problems. I learned from her that hard work, determination, and a strong sense of purpose are essential to achieving our goals. She instilled in us that we should never give up or let our circumstances defeat us. Her resilience and consistency in the face of adversity taught me to stay focused on what's important and to prioritize my goals, even when things get tough. I have carried her strength with me through my own life experience and entrepreneurial journey.

As entrepreneurs, we can use our experiences with trauma to fuel our creativity and innovation. We can use our pain to create solutions that make a difference in the world. But we must prioritize our emotional well-being and seek support when needed. We must also recognize that our trauma does not define us, and it does not have to control our lives.

Multiple Streams of Income

As an entrepreneur, I've learned that having multiple streams of income is essential. "Over the years", I've been involved in various businesses, and each has taught me valuable lessons. I'll share some of these lessons and the experiences that have shaped my journey.

Lesson 1: Know the Industry

The first lesson I want to share is the importance of knowing knowing the industry you're going into. When you understand the laws and regulations that govern the industry, you can make informed decisions that can help you avoid costly mistakes. It's also essential to stay current with information about the industry. As an entrepreneur, you never stop learning, and you must always be a lifelong student.

I learned this lesson the hard way from my first business, which was an income tax business. Initially, things were booming, but after fifteen years, I became complacent and wasn't keeping up with my due diligence, which consisted of making sure that my clients had the necessary documentation that was required for certain tax credits they were expected to be eligible for. This oversight taught me an incredibly valuable lesson about ensuring I knew how to educate my clients for success. I recognized that knowledge is power which inspired me, this gave me the idea to create my very own franchise, *Prestige Income Tax in a Box*. This happens to be one of the first female African American home-based income tax franchises in the United States which allows entrepreneurs to get into the income tax industry, while teaching them how to properly protect themselves from due diligence discrepancies.

Lesson 2: Know When to Pivot

As an entrepreneur, it's important to be flexible and willing to pivot when external changes impact your business. Even the most successful plans can become obsolete in the face of shifting markets, emerging technologies, or other unforeseen circumstances. Knowing when to pivot can be the difference between staying relevant and profitable or becoming obsolete and irrelevant.

For example, my experience as a landlord in the real estate industry taught me the importance of being open to new opportunities. When I realized that the market was changing rapidly, I knew I needed to adapt to stay successful. Instead of continuing to focus solely on being a landlord, I decided to pivot and explore other ways to stay in the industry that I love, which led me to the idea of "Flipping Houses". I had previously purchased a multi-unit property as a means to generate passive income. Unfortunately, the business relationship between my general contractor and myself didn't work out and we decided to part ways. Typically, this would be a major setback. However, I had taken a more hands on approach with my other investment property, that I was attempting to flip while the other project was going on. My desire to learn coupled with being hands-on made me comfortable to pivot by obtaining my own general contractor's license to handle the project myself. This pivot taught me the importance of having the courage to make tough decisions and take calculated risks to stay successful as an entrepreneur.

Lesson 3: Seize the Moment

The third lesson I want to share is the importance of seizing opportunities when they arise. This is something that I learned firsthand when I was a young adult and got into the landscaping industry by running my dad's business. One day, while working at my job, a neighbor approached me with an opportunity to manage bank-owned properties. At that time, the shapewear industry, which I was involved in, was losing momentum, and becoming over saturated. I saw this as a chance to diversify my entrepreneurial portfolio and generate additional income while honoring my late father's legacy and expertise in landscaping.

By seizing the moment and taking advantage of the opportunity presented to me, I was able to grow and expand my business beyond what I had ever imagined. It taught me that it's important to be open to new opportunities and act on them when they come along, even if it means taking a risk or stepping outside of your comfort zone. It's important to stay aware of your surroundings and be ready to act when an opportunity arises, even if it means venturing into new territory

Lesson 4: The Power of Multiplying Your Business

When I was in my early 20s, I gained valuable experience in

the tax preparation industry by running my stepmother's franchise tax office. When I opened my own office, I invited my friends and family to become tax agents, which allowed them to learn the business and become their own bosses. Through this experience, I learned the importance of multiplying your business by sharing your knowledge and expertise.

To multiply your business, it's essential to focus on creating value for others. By sharing your knowledge and expertise, you can help others achieve success in their own ventures, which in turn can lead to more business for you. This multiplier effect is incredibly powerful and can help you achieve exponential growth in your business. Through my experience, I came to realize that helping others helped me expand my reach. By helping other people get into the tax preparation business, I was able to serve more people and make more money. This experience taught me the power of expanding my business by sharing my knowledge and the multiplier effect it had.

The franchise strategy is one of the best multiplier business strategies. By offering a turnkey solution, I helped others replicate my success while also generating additional revenue through franchise fees and royalties. The expansion ultimately served more clients, as it created opportunities for others to become their own bosses and achieve financial independence.

In addition to franchising, there are many other ways to multiply your business, such as creating training programs, collaborating with others, building a referral network, or creating content. The key is to identify ways to share your knowledge and expertise with others, while also creating value for them and yourself. By doing so, you can achieve exponential growth in your business and help others achieve success on their own.

Lesson 5: Don't Be Afraid to Sell Your By-product

The fifth lesson I want to share is one I was reminded of by my publisher Dr. Joan Wright-Good. It is, knowing the importance of not being afraid to sell your byproduct. When I started my shapewear business, only a few celebrities were in that space, which were Keyshia Ka'Oir and Premadonna. I saw this as an opportunity to get in front of the market and take advantage of a gap in the industry. My shapewear business quickly took off and I noticed that many of my customers were looking for a more permanent solution.

At the time noninvasive body contouring procedures were not readily available to the everyday woman. I wanted to provide those services to my clients, so I pursued the proper certification. By doing this I built credibility with my clients which allowed me to find additional products and services that met their needs. My clients would ask me what else they could do to maintain their desired results. That led me to begin selling wellness supplements. Unbeknownst to me this investment proved to be valuable. When Covid hit it was one of the few of my businesses that was negatively impacted. Although I had to close my body contouring business the supplement business allowed me to continue generating revenue. Although I had to close my body contouring business the supplement business allowed me to continue generating revenue. As an entrepreneur, you have to know when it's the right time to sell your byproduct. This experience taught me to always look for ways to maximize the value of my business.

Lesson 6: Look for a Silver Lining

The lessons that I've learned in life have helped prepare me for the unexpected, like the Coronavirus Pandemic. During this global crisis, many people were losing their lives and the government was struggling to manage lockdowns and other measures to protect public health. However, I was able to find a silver lining and create something positive out of this difficult situation.

Together with my best friend, we created the Prosperity Testing Center to test individuals and keep families safe. It was a great feeling to be able to provide a stream of income while helping to protect the community. Our center helped keep people safe and gave them peace of mind during an uncertain time. It was an opportunity to turn a challenging situation into a positive outcome. I am grateful for the lessons I've learned and for the opportunity to apply them during the pandemic. The experience has taught me to look for silver linings in all situations, and to use my creativity and resourcefulness to create positive change.

Overall, these lessons have shaped my journey as an entrepreneur and have allowed me to develop multiple streams of income. Knowing the industry, being willing to pivot, seizing the moment, multiplying my business, and not being afraid to sell my byproduct are all crucial components of a successful entrepreneurial journey. Continuously learning, adapting, and expanding my business, I have been able to stay relevant and profitable in an ever-changing market.

The Lesson

So, what is the takeaway here? I started my story by telling you about the men in my life. I'll end my story with me. My change started with me. Once I began to prioritize my own self-care, and journey of growth I was able to mentally bounce back from my personal crisis and learn from all the lessons life was teaching me. Every lesson always came back to me finding my voice. I needed to find my voice in my marriage, after my divorce, and throughout my life. I literally needed to find my voice, which came after being diagnosed with Expressive Language Disorder. After being frustrated for so long not understanding how to relay my words and thoughts, it was a relief to know there was a reason for it all.

I began to understand my diagnosis and do the work to master my communication while regaining my voice. I chose to look at each mistake as a valuable lesson, and what I once called scars became the healed wounds of a survivor, overcomer, and successful entrepreneur. Just like me you have greatness inside of you.

Be The "Boss Chic" You Were Created to Be

So go out there and be the bad chic that you are. Follow your dreams, no matter how long it takes. Use every obstacle and mistake as a lesson creating a blueprint for you to find your path. I hope in reading my story you will be motivated to endure the trials and tribulations that come with life and entrepreneurship. What I thought was wasted time and me being unmotivated was me finding my space in this world. As someone who made it out, I'm holding space for you.

Be The "Boss Chic" You Were Created to Be

I am in a new place in my life right now. I am forty-four years old, and in a healthy loving relationship with an amazing man who supports me as a partner and in business. We are in the process of trying to have a baby. I am currently undergoing fertility treatments to complete my dream of having a child. My faith in God has seen me through in the past, so I know for sure He will see me through this next stage of my life as well.

He created me, so now I live life with purpose, on purpose, for purpose. I have found love, and I am grateful. I'm always adding additional streams of income with the latest being, a couple short term rental partnerships, also an online learning platform called "Serial Entrepreneur Academy" and a podcast called "Multi Level Money" where we talk about entrepreneurship. I have finally found happiness. Don't forget it's not about the path you take but the journey along the "way". Embrace Life!

Here are a few quotes that helped me during my toughest seasons. I hope they help you to rise to the occasion too.

"We may encounter many defeats, but we must not be defeated."
Maya Angelou

"If there is no struggle, there is no progress."
Frederick Douglass

"Do not fear failure, but rather fear not trying."
Roy T. Bennett

"If you can't fly, then run, if you can't run, then walk, if you can't walk, then crawl, but whatever you do, you have to

keep moving forward."
Martin Luther King Jr.

"Every time you state what you want or believe, you're the first to hear it. It's a message to both you and others about what you think is possible. Don't put a ceiling on yourself." Oprah Winfrey

"Life has two rules. Number one: never quit! Number two: always remember rule number one."
Duke Ellington

TAKE SOME TIME TO REFLECT ON THIS SECTION AND NOTATE SOME ACTIONABLE POINTS

Where can we connect?

If you want to learn more ways on becoming a serial entrepreneur, check out my website,

Serial Entrepreneur Academy
www.serialentrepreneuracademy.com

You'll find a variety of educational step by step courses and resources to help you on your journey.

Be sure to tune in to my podcast *Multi Level Money with Stephanie Elise* that's available on
Apple Music, Pandora, Amazon Audible, Spotify and Iheart

Connect with me on Instagram @iamstephanieelise

Visit me online at https://stephanieelise.info

Sometimes when you follow your dream, it opens the door for others to be able to follow theirs."

Thanks for your support.

BOOK DESCRIPTION

All the statements you've heard about money when you were younger remain in your subconscious until you become older. It then become part of the blueprint that lays the foundation for your financial life.

What this means is that, wherever you are right now financially is heavily dependent on your blueprint. If you are not where you want to be, you must move to a higher level of abundance mindset, you must be willing to let go of some of the old ways of thinking and adopt new ones. Girl, there's no excuse is the resource you never knew you needed. It is the ultimate tool to help you adopt a new money mindset.

The authors, Keayna, Stephanie, and Natalie, authentically shared from a wealth of experience and knowledge.

The vast majority of people simply do not have the internal tools to create wealth on their own especially with the increased challenges of going through a pandemic and a recession. The authors took these challenges into consideration as they labored on this assignment.

These three ladies are living examples and proof that; success comes from persistently improving and inventing oneself and the gift they've been given. It does not come from persistently doing what's not working. In the same breath, business is not just about money, but about making dreams come true for others while creating a true legacy for yourself. In other words, creating a business is a great way to improve the world while improving yourself.

www.ingramcontent.com/pod-product-compliance
Lightning Source LLC
Chambersburg PA
CBHW050705160426
43194CB00010B/2007